AIRCRAFT

Amazing Agricultural Aircraft

Timothy R. Gaffney

Enslow Publishers, Inc.

40 Industrial Road   PO Box 38
Box 398   Aldershot
Berkeley Heights, NJ 07922   Hants GU12 6BP
USA   UK
http://www.enslow.com

Library of Congress Cataloging-in-Publication Data

Gaffney, Timothy R.
Amazing agricultural aircraft / Timothy R. Gaffney.
     p. cm. — (Aircraft)
    Includes bibliographical references (p.) and index.
    ISBN 0-7660-1608-0 (hardcover)
    1. Aeronautics in agriculture—Juvenile literature. 2. Private planes—
Juvenile literature. 3. Helicopters—Juvenile literature. [1. Aeronautics in
agriculture. 2. Airplanes.] I. Title.
S494.5.A3 G34 2001
632'.94—dc21

                                             00-011207

Printed in the United States of America

10 9 8 7 6 5 4 3 2 1

To Our Readers: We have done our best to make sure all Internet addresses in
this book were active and appropriate when we went to press. However, the author
and the publisher have no control over and assume no liability for the material
available on those Internet sites or on other Web sites they may link to. Any
comments or suggestions can be sent by e-mail to comments@enslow.com or to
the address on the back cover.

Photo Credits: Mabry Anderson, pp. 14, 18, 21; © Corel Corporation, pp. 3,
12, 22, 29, 40; Delta Heritage Museum, p. 16; David G. Fitzgerald, pp. 4–5,
10, 26, 36, 38, 39; Timothy R. Gaffney, pp. 7, 8, 23, 24, 27, 28, 30, 31, 33, 34.

Cover Photo: David G. Fitzgerald

Contents

1 A Flash of Wings 4

2 The Crop Dusters 12

3 Designed for the Job 22

4 The Modern Ag Plane 29

5 Helicopters 40

Chapter Notes 43

Glossary 46

Further Reading and
    Internet Addresses 47

Index 48

CHAPTER 1

A Flash of Wings

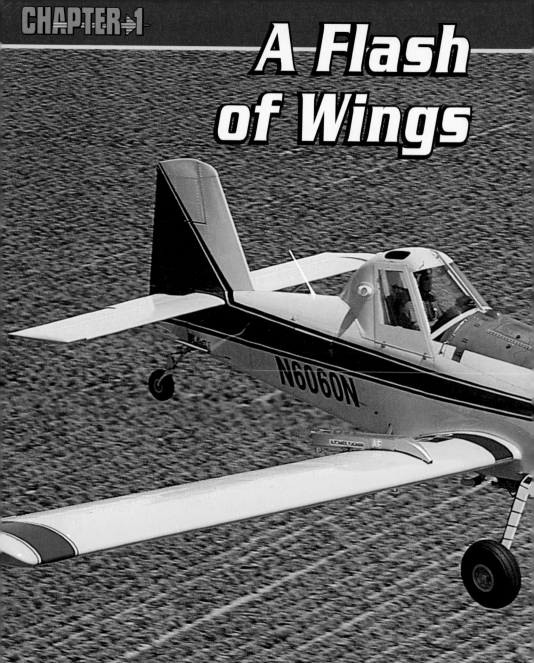

Air Tractor AT-402B

*L*ost in a daydream in the family car, you barely notice the green farm fields that stretch endlessly into the distance on both sides of the highway. But a sudden, snarling roar and a flash of yellow against the blue sky blasts you loose from your thoughts.

You strain against your seat belt to press your face against the car window. There it is: a spread of yellow wings close overhead, moving fast. An airplane has just popped up from the field along the highway. It is only there for an instant as it climbs and banks sharply, wings almost straight up and down. The image of an ancient-looking flying machine is burned in your mind: big and beefy, with two sets of wings and a tail as big as a barn door. But it is surprisingly swift and nimble as it turns.

It dives back toward the field and levels out just above the crops. A white mist begins to spread from beneath its lower wings. Away it races, trailing the mist across the green field, flying fast and close to the ground.

What was that? You know about airliners that carry passengers across the ceiling of the sky. You know about military fighters and bombers. This was different, like something from another world.

In a sense, it was. It was an airplane from the seldom-seen world of agricultural aviation. Agricultural airplanes and helicopters work in rural areas, where there are few people to see them. They spray chemicals on farm fields to fertilize soil and to control harmful plants and insects. They also spread seeds for rice and some other crops.

Agricultural pilots—or ag pilots, as most call themselves—fly at racecar speeds just a few feet above the ground. Whipping into a steep turn at the end of each pass, they put on a low-level air show for the plants they treat. There are no air show crowds to cheer and wave,

Pilot Joe Vick demonstrates how his Ag-Cat B-600 sprays crops or soil.

but ag pilots do not fly to impress others. They love the excitement of going low and fast.

"There's a rush going across a field at 150 miles an hour, five feet above the ground," says Robert McCurdy, who teaches agricultural flying at Northeast Louisiana University in Monroe, Louisiana. "I've been doing it for thirty-some years, and I love it."[1]

The work takes quick reflexes, lots of practice, and total concentration. McCurdy says an ag pilot always has to watch for trees, power lines, or other obstacles that can kill a pilot in a heartbeat. For instance, he says, "We fly under [power-line] wires because it's safer to fly under them than to try to jump them."

Every year, agricultural aircraft seed, fertilize, and chemically treat 468,750 square miles of U.S. farmland—more land area than California and Texas combined. Aircraft spray about a quarter of all the chemicals used to kill insects on U.S. farms. Almost all rice grown in the United States is seeded by air.[2]

Aircraft are important tools because they can seed or spray a field much more quickly and efficiently than tractors or other ground equipment, according to Lynn Carlson of Northfield, Minnesota. An ag pilot, Carlson was also president of the National Agricultural Aviation

The Ag-Cat B-600 flies toward traffic on Interstate 70 in Ohio. Ag pilots fly close to the ground and must be alert for obstructions—even cars and trucks.

Association in 2000. He says aircraft can treat wet fields that are too soft for tractors, and they do not pack down the soil or trample plants.[3]

But a rare, fleeting glimpse of yellow wings is all you might see of an ag airplane. Only about 6,000 airplanes and 400 helicopters across the United States are used in agriculture.[4] That is a small fraction of the 192,400 general aviation aircraft in use today.[5] (*General aviation* is the term used to describe all aircraft besides airliners and military aircraft. It includes agricultural aircraft.) Even people who live in farm country might not be aware of aviation's role in farming today.

Carlson recalls his experience at an air show in rural Minnesota. "I had my [agricultural] airplane there. I was surprised at the people who didn't realize we still [treated crops by air]. It was kind of a shocker for me."[6]

You may never have seen an agricultural airplane or helicopter at work, but you probably have seen the results: supermarket shelves loaded with fruits and vegetables. Agricultural aviation may well have had a hand in growing the grain for your breakfast cereal. Cheese, milk, beef, and pork come from animals that may have fed on crops grown with the help of aircraft. Many non-food crops, such as cotton and trees, are also treated by air.[7]

Agricultural aviation grew rapidly following the end of World War II in 1945. Many new insect- and weed-killing chemicals were invented, and airplanes could cover large areas quickly. In the 1950s, the U.S.

Agricultural aircraft play a large role in farming. This Air Tractor plane is spraying a field of cabbage with chemicals.

government hired ag pilots to spray millions of acres at a time in campaigns to wipe out insect pests. Airplanes sprayed fields, forests, streams, and towns.

But scientific studies found the widespread use of these chemicals also hurt birds, land animals, and fish that were exposed to them. The peregrine falcon is one of many species that shrank in number.[8] Scientist Rachel Carson criticized the huge spraying programs in her 1962 book *Silent Spring*. In it, she wrote, the chemicals affected "not only the target insect or plant, but anything" they touched.[9] Carson's book made many people aware of the issue and forced the government to pay more attention to safety.

Today, the government more closely controls the use of agricultural chemicals. Aerial spraying is done more sparingly and carefully. Aircraft and spray systems are better, and pilots get more training in the proper use of chemicals.

The use of aircraft to lay down chemicals is still the preferred method in certain conditions, according to Ivan W. Kirk, an agricultural engineer with the U.S. Department of Agriculture in College Station, Texas. Kirk, who studies the use of agricultural aviation, says it is the best method available when fields must be treated quickly, when the area to be treated is large, or when fields are difficult to get into, such as rice fields that are normally flooded.

More work is needed to make aerial spraying safer and more effective, Kirk says, but he thinks agricultural pilots are still an important part of modern farming: "They provide a service or commodity that is in demand—that is why we still have them."[10]

Agricultural pilots today know they have to be more careful with chemicals, Lynn Carlson says. "Now, you have to be much more aware of the environment, more aware of the chemicals. [You have to] know which chemicals will work best on the weeds, the [proper] spray rates. . . . There's more involved than just flying an aircraft."[11]

CHAPTER 2

The Crop Dusters

Early agricultural pilots dusted fields with dry chemicals, mainly to kill insects. People called them crop dusters. The nickname is still widely used, but it is outdated because modern ag pilots mainly spray liquid chemicals. Some modern ag pilots resent the old nickname because they believe it carries a bad image of devil-may-care pilots in ragged old airplanes.

In truth, agricultural aviation has a history almost as old as aviation itself.

The first experiment in spreading chemicals by air came on August 31, 1921, less than eighteen years after the beginning of powered flight. In that experiment, the U.S. Department of

Agriculture teamed up with the Army Air Service to turn an old training plane into the first crop duster.

The airplane was a Curtiss JN-6H Jenny. Like most airplanes in those days, it was a biplane, meaning it had two sets of wings. The army had used Jenny airplanes to train military pilots for World War I. At the army's McCook Field in Dayton, Ohio, an engineer named Etienne Darmoy built a hopper to hold dry chemicals and bolted it to the Jenny's side. A hopper is a container with an opening, usually at the bottom, from which its contents can be emptied at a specific rate. The hopper was filled with lead arsenate powder, an insect-killing chemical.

On the day of the test, Darmoy climbed into the rear cockpit, where he would work the hopper. An army test pilot, Lieutenant John Macready, climbed into the front. They took off and quickly flew to a grove of catalpa trees about ten miles away. The trees were infested with the larvae of the Catalpa Sphinx Moth, an insect that could strip the trees of their leaves.

Macready estimated how much the dust would drift in the wind. Then he aimed the Jenny at the grove. He roared across it just eight or ten feet above the treetops while Darmoy turned a crank to release the chemical. The propeller blast and the wake of the speeding plane fanned the powder across the trees.

"We could see from the airplane that the dust was spreading in the right place," Macready recalled in a letter. In just a few passes, they finished what would have taken hours on the ground. After they landed, Macready

One of the original Curtiss JN-6 Jenny Dusters is doing the first dusting ever on cotton, near Tallulah, Louisiana, in August 1922.

wrote that the Department of Agriculture people "were so breathless and excited they could barely talk. . . . What had been a very big thing to them had been a short, easy flying job for us."[1]

The successful test increased interest in the use of airplanes for agriculture. More tests were flown in 1922 and 1923 near Tallulah, Louisiana. Researchers found airplanes useful for treating fruit and nut trees, vegetables, grains, and grasses. They were especially useful for spreading chemicals to fight the boll weevil, a beetle that attacks cotton plants.

In the early 1920s, the Huff-Daland Aero Corporation of Ogdensburg, New York, began making crop-dusting airplanes. It did this by adding a hopper to an airplane it was already making. Huff-Daland called its new airplanes Dusters. The company made crop dusting international: In 1927, Huff-Daland shipped seven Dusters to Peru to fight boll weevils.

Crop-dusting companies were springing up around the United States by the mid-1920s. One, the Delta Aero Dusters of Monroe, Louisiana, operated a fleet of crop-dusting airplanes. The company also started a passenger service. It grew and changed into a passenger airline that is famous today: Delta Air Lines.[2]

The Sturdy Stearman

During World War II, thousands of military pilots learned to fly in the rugged, reliable Boeing Stearman. The Stearman has two open cockpits, one in front of the other. Between 1938 and 1944, the Boeing Company built more than 8,500 Stearmans and enough spare parts to build 2,000 more.[3]

Like many older airplanes, Stearmans have radial engines. Pilots sometimes call them "big round engines" because their cylinders are arranged in a circle around the central crankshaft. (Engine cylinders contain pistons that move back and forth, pushing rods connected to the crankshaft. The rods make the crankshaft turn, and the crankshaft turns the propeller.)[4]

An early Huff Daland plane applies calcium arsenate on cotton plants in 1924.

After the war ended in 1945, the U.S. Army and Navy had thousands of Stearmans they no longer needed and sold them cheaply. An ag pilot could buy a Stearman for a few hundred dollars. He could turn it into a crop duster by mounting a hopper in the front cockpit and a dusting or spraying system under the lower wing. A simple tube could release dry chemicals. For spraying liquids, pilots mounted a spray boom under the bottom wing. The spray boom was a long pipe with a row of nozzles.

Not only was the Stearman cheap, it was a good airplane for the job. In some ways, it set the standard for future ag airplanes.

- It had a strong frame of welded steel tubing that protected the pilot in a crash.

- It was stable in level flight, but it could turn quickly. This allowed pilots to fly straight, close rows back and forth across a field, with quick, tight turns at the end of each row.

- Its two sets of wings worked like one very large wing: They produced a lot of lift. This helped the Stearman take off in a short distance.

- Its rugged landing gear let it land on rough ground. Ag pilots could land on a short, unpaved airstrip near the fields they were spraying, load up with chemicals, and take off again.

- The Stearman's wings also gave it what pilots call a gentle stall.

When an airplane stalls, it means its wings stop making lift. A wing makes lift with a curved upper surface that forces air to flow faster over the wing than under it. The faster-moving air has less pressure than the air under the wing. The air under the wing pushes up, and the result is what pilots call lift. If the airflow over the wing gets too slow, or if the angle of the wing to the airflow

A lineup of Stearman biplanes in the 1950s. Ag pilots turned Stearmans into ag planes. They added a hopper to the front cockpit and a dusting or spraying system under the lower wing.

gets too steep and causes the airflow to get rough, then the pressure over the wing will increase, and the wing will lose its lift: It will stall.[5]

When an airplane stalls, it will drop toward the ground. Pilots are trained to recover a stalled airplane by lowering the nose to get the air flowing smoothly again.[6] But not all airplanes behave alike when they stall. In some airplanes, the pilot has to point the nose down sharply. That can be deadly for a pilot flying just a few feet above the ground. The Stearman needs just a little nose-down movement. It allows pilots to recover from a stall without losing too much altitude.[7]

Bigger Engines, Bigger Loads

Ag pilots bought the leftover Stearmans by the thousands.[8] To make the planes able to carry heavier loads, they put 450-horsepower engines on them—more than double the power of their original engines. The bigger engine made the Stearman a real workhorse. According to the National Agricultural Aviation Museum, "The Stearman was the cornerstone of the crop-dusting industry."[9]

To a crop duster, nothing sounded finer than the rumble of a big radial engine. Nothing looked more beautiful than a sunrise viewed through a pair of wings. And nothing felt more exciting than diving down at a green field, leveling off at the last second, and screaming across the ground so low and fast that the crop rows flashed into a blur. For most crop dusters, the affordable, rugged Stearman was the airplane that made their livelihood possible.

At the same time, flying the open-cockpit biplanes day in and day out was hard work. The constant roar of the engine, propeller, and wind was mind-numbing. The chemicals stank, and the vibrating engines shook the pilot constantly. "When I started flying ag planes, I flew Stearmans," Robert McCurdy said. "If you put nine or ten hours in one of those planes in a day, you were mentally and physically exhausted."[10]

As the Stearmans wore out and the use of airplanes in agriculture grew, airplane companies saw a market for a new kind of specialty airplane: the ag plane. Several companies began selling ag planes in the 1950s and early 1960s.

As newer airplanes came on the scene, the Stearman's role as a crop duster faded. Today, Stearmans are most likely seen flying at air shows. One of the best-known air show teams, the Red Baron Pizza Squadron, flies Stearmans that were converted from crop dusters.[11]

Specifications for
Stearman
(basic models)[12]

Primary function—Military training plane

Manufacturer—Boeing

Wingspan—32 feet 2 inches

Length—25 feet ¼ inch

Height—9 feet 2 inches

Empty weight—1,936 pounds

Maximum weight—2,717–2,810 pounds

Maximum power—215–225 horsepower (original engines)

Maximum speed—120–126 miles per hour

Range—440–505 miles

Maximum altitude—11,200 feet above sea level

CHAPTER 3

Designed for the Job

One glance tells you the Ag-Cat was not made for beauty. Big and brawny, the Ag-Cat was made for hard work on the farm. It looks tough, and it is.

"They're extremely strong, very ruggedly built, and they can operate out of some of the most difficult places to land," says Robert McCurdy.[1]

Like the Stearman, the Ag-Cat is a biplane. It might look old-fashioned, but the Ag-Cat was born in the jet age. It was one of the first airplanes designed from scratch for agricultural aviation.

Why such a funny name? The Ag-Cat was designed by the Grumman Aircraft Corporation. Grumman had a tradition of

The tough Grumman Ag-Cat sits outside its hangar. The cockpit hatch is open on the left side.

naming its combat planes after fierce cats—Hellcat, Tigercat, and Wildcat, for example. Following that tradition, Grumman named this agricultural airplane the Ag-Cat.

Setting the Standard

The Ag-Cat design includes the best features of the Stearman and some that the Stearman lacked. The Ag-Cat helped set the standard for modern ag planes.

Its rugged steel frame includes special crash protection for the pilot. The cockpit has a metal cage, or frame, to protect the pilot if the airplane crash-lands upside down. Metals used in the frame were carefully chosen for their ability to resist corrosion from harsh farm chemicals. Corrosion could weaken a frame and cause a crash.

The pilot sits high to get a good view ahead and to the sides. (The first Ag-Cats had open cockpits. Later ones enclosed the pilot to protect him or her from the chemicals.)

The hopper is located between the pilot and the engine, at a balance point between the nose and the tail. In this location, thousands of pounds of material can be loaded and sprayed out without changing the airplane's balance. Without this balance, the airplane could become hard to control as its weight changes.

Joe Vick, an ag pilot who lives near Columbus, Ohio, owns two Ag-Cats. He said he and his father started flying them in the 1970s because they were operating

The cockpit of the Ag-Cat B-600 has a metal frame to protect the pilot if the airplane makes a crash landing upside down.

from a short, rough airstrip. They chose the Ag-Cat because it could haul a lot of weight off short strips, and its rugged landing gear could handle rough surfaces.

Vick especially loves his Ag-Cat B-600. Its 600-horsepower engine has more than twice the power of the original Ag-Cat's 250-horsepower engine, and its wings are six feet longer, which provides much more lift to carry more weight. Its hopper can hold 300 gallons of liquid—more than a ton. "It's just a dream to fly. You don't ever have to worry about overloading it," Vick says. "And they turn so well. Unless you're flying [an airplane with] a high-power turbine [engine], nothing turns as well as an Ag-Cat."[2]

Despite its old-fashioned looks, the Ag-Cat can be as accurate as the most modern ag planes with the use of space technology. Like many ag pilots today, Vick uses satellite navigation to make his spraying patterns precise.

Space-age Tools

Ag pilots need to avoid overlapping or missing rows on their passes. If they overlap, some plants will get sprayed twice, wasting chemical and possibly damaging the plants. If they miss, some plants will get no treatment at all.

Over the years, ag pilots have used different methods to line up their passes. Many used flaggers. These were people who stood at each end of a row and held up a pole with a flag on it. Later, an airplane-mounted device called an Automatic Flagman allowed a pilot to mark the end of a row by dropping out a paper flag.

Ag pilots have used different methods to line up over a field of crops. Here, a flagger stands at the end of a row to direct the pilot of an Air Tractor aircraft.

Now ag pilots have a space-age tool known as the Global Positioning System, or GPS. This is a network of satellites that transmits radio signals for navigation. In Vick's Ag-Cats, a GPS receiver—a radio with a built-in computer—checks the signals of several GPS satellites to calculate the airplane's position within several feet. Additional signals from ground-based transmitters fine-tune the receiver's accuracy to within a few inches. With a GPS receiver, Vick can tell exactly where he needs to fly to avoid overlapping or missing parts of an agricultural field.

Joe Vick's Ag-Cat sits outside its hangar. The radial engine is large and powerful.

Most Ag-Cats were built with radial engines. "I compare the Ag-Cat to the Harley Davidson," says Robert McCurdy. The Harley is a classic motorcycle known for the deep, rhythmic beat of its engine. "If I were going to ride a motorcycle from here to California, I would ride a Honda Gold Wing. But if somebody were going to give me a motorcycle, I would want a Harley."[3]

The Ag-Cat is still popular with pilots who need a rugged airplane that can haul 400-gallon loads off short, rough airstrips. But a newer generation of larger, faster ag planes has taken over most of the work.

Specifications for Ag-Cat B-600[4]

Primary function—Agriculture

Manufacturer—Grumman, Schweizer

Wingspan—Top, 42 feet 2 ¾ inches;
Bottom, 40 feet 6 ¾ inches

Length—25 feet 7 inches

Height—11 feet

Empty weight—3,250 pounds

Maximum weight—4,500 pounds

Maximum power—600 horsepower

Hopper capacity—300 gallons (2,200 pounds)

Fuel capacity—80 gallons

Maximum speed—147 miles per hour

Stall speed—54 miles per hour

Maximum rate of climb—2,000 feet per
minute empty

Range—Approximately 300 miles

CHAPTER 4

The Modern Ag Plane

The sky is clear and the air is calm on a morning in May at the Gibbses' country residence near Fremont, Ohio. The morning is silent except for an occasional car or truck passing on the country road. Soon a purr rises in the sky and Luther Gibbs Jr.'s yellow airplane flashes into sight, turning low over the end of their grass airstrip. He sets the plane down and taxis to a gravel-covered pad next to a hangar near the house. He swings the plane around, sets the brake, and climbs out.

The airplane has one set of wings. Its nose is long and narrow. Its idling engine sounds like a loud vacuum cleaner. Gibbs's father,

Luther Gibbs Jr.'s sleek yellow Air Tractor has one set of wings. The spray boom under the wing of this AT-400 is clearly visible.

Luther Sr., drags a hose to the plane and begins pumping fuel into the tanks.

An assistant hooks another hose to a valve under the plane's belly. He pumps a chemical for killing alfalfa weevils into the plane's hopper. Then he adds water. The water thins the chemical to the proper mixture. It also flushes the hose and valve clean. When the hose comes off, if anything drips out, it will only be water.

The men do not hurry, but they work quickly and efficiently. An airplane sitting on the ground is not working, the elder Gibbs explains. "Time on the ground is

A hose refills the hopper of an AT-400 with liquid insecticide.

lost time," he says. "We try to get it back in the air as quickly as we can."[1]

Soon the airplane is refueled and its hopper filled. The younger Gibbs climbs back into the plane and puts on his safety helmet. He checks a list for the next job. He revs up the propeller, taxis down to the far end of the runway, turns, and adds power. The plane is quickly airborne. It roars past the hangar, just clearing a row of trees and the power lines that run along the road. Then it banks into a turn and flies out of sight. About a half hour later Gibbs returns for another refill.

≡ Bigger Farms, Bigger Planes

Luther Gibbs Sr. started a tomato spraying business in 1952. For years he used ground-based spraying equipment that had to be set up in the fields. As farms got larger and the areas dedicated to single crops grew, Gibbs says, farmers needed a way to spray fields quickly to control fast-spreading insects. Gibbs turned to airplanes.

He hired a pilot in 1967 to do aerial spraying, but the pilot was also a full-time firefighter. He always seemed to be at his firefighting job when the weather was right for spraying. Already a private pilot, Gibbs decided in 1969 to become his own ag pilot. He bought a small ag plane called a Piper Pawnee. It had a single pair of wings and a 250-horsepower engine. Later, Luther Jr. began flying. The Gibbses added another small ag plane called a Cessna Ag Wagon.

Luther Gibbs, Jr., prepares for another flight in his Air Tractor AT-400. He wears a safety helmet and harness.

The elder Gibbs decided to retire from ag flying in 1991 and let Luther Jr. start running the business. "When my dad wanted to retire, I either had to hire somebody or do more myself," Gibbs says. "That's why I bought this airplane."[2]

Gibbs bought an Air Tractor AT-400. Its 400-gallon hopper dwarfs the capacities of the Pawnee and the Ag

The AT-400's turboprop engine provides the power needed to run this aircraft. Here, the Air Tractor lands on a grass strip.

Wagon. "It would take me three loads with the old Pawnee to do what I do with one load in the Air Tractor," Gibbs says. It also does the job faster. Gibbs races across fields at 140 miles an hour. "The old Pawnee only goes about ninety."

The AT-400 gets its power from a turboprop engine. Instead of using pistons to turn a propeller, a turboprop works much like a jet. The engine burns a mixture of compressed air and fuel and forces the hot exhaust gas out the back. In a regular jet engine, the exhaust gas produces most of the thrust that pushes the airplane forward. In a turboprop, the exhaust gas passes through a turbine, which uses a system of gears to turn a propeller.[3]

Turboprop engines are much more expensive than piston engines, but Gibbs says they weigh less and produce more power. This allows an airplane to carry a heavier load. Their narrower shape allows the airplane's nose to be more streamlined, which lets it go faster. Turboprop planes can be run longer between overhauls, which means they can keep working while airplanes with piston engines might be in the repair shop. They also run smoother, which means less noise and vibration for the pilot.

Luther Gibbs Jr.'s operation reflects today's trend in agricultural aviation. A smaller number of ag pilots are doing the same amount of work as in earlier years with bigger, faster, and more efficient airplanes.[4]

"The name of the game in ag aviation today is speed and comfort and load carrying. The bigger planes are much faster," says Robert McCurdy.[5] The Air Tractor line of ag planes is a good example.

Air Tractors

Based in Olney, Texas, Air Tractor Inc. claims to be the world's biggest producer of ag planes today. Air Tractors come in a wide range of sizes. Gibbs's AT-400 is an older model. Equipped with a 400-gallon hopper, it is as small as any ag plane Air Tractor makes today.

The hopper of the Air Tractor AT-802 is lowered into the plane. The hopper can carry up to 820 gallons.

Air Tractor's biggest model is the AT-802A. It is so big that Air Tractor used the same basic design to make a sister model, the AT-802F, for fighting wildfires. Both models can carry up to 820 gallons in their hoppers, or more than 6,500 pounds. While the AT-802A gently sprays crops, the AT-802F can drench a wildfire at a controlled rate or dump its whole load in seconds.

Compared to the Ag-Cat, McCurdy says, "An ag plane today is a 911 Porsche [sports car] with wings." The controls on newer turboprop airplanes are like power steering, he says: light to the touch and very responsive. "These airplanes are as nimble as a ballet dancer."[6]

Air Tractor still makes one model, the AT-401B, with a radial engine. It is the sister of the turboprop-powered AT-402A and AT-402B. The few radial engine models that are made are sold mainly to customers in other countries, Air Tractor spokeswoman Kristin Snow says.

A radial engine model is much cheaper to buy—about $240,000 for an AT-401B, compared to $400,000 for a turboprop-powered AT-402A. Air Tractor's biggest ag plane, the AT-802A, cost nearly $1 million in 2000. Even so, Snow says, "most of our sales are [turboprop] because they are more reliable, faster, [and] more productive."[7]

The five-blade propeller of the AT-802 looms large in this shot of the company's biggest agricultural plane.

Specifications for
Air Tractor AT-802[8]

Primary function—Agriculture, firefighting

Manufacturer—Air Tractor Inc.

Wingspan—59.2 feet

Length—36 feet

Height—11 feet

Empty weight—6,505 pounds

Maximum weight—16,000 pounds

Maximum power—1,350 horsepower

Hopper capacity—820 gallons
(6,560 pounds of water)

Fuel capacity—254 gallons

Maximum speed—221 miles per hour

Stall speed—92 miles per hour

Range—800 miles

CHAPTER 5

Helicopters

Since the first crop-dusting experiment in 1921, many kinds of aircraft have been designed or changed for agriculture. This includes helicopters as well as airplanes.

Helicopters fly the same way airplanes do: They use wings for lift. The spinning blades on a helicopter are actually wings. Instead of being fixed, like airplane wings, rotating helicopter wings get lift when they move through the air. Rapidly spinning rotor blades create enough lift to allow a helicopter to go straight up or hover.

Helicopters were not widely used until after World War II. After 1945, a few companies began building helicopters with the idea that people would fly them for everyday use, just like cars. But helicopters are more difficult to fly than cars are to drive, and they are much more expensive. Helicopter makers needed to find other uses for them.

Bell Helicopter found it hard to sell its small, two-seat Model 47 in the late 1940s. The company altered the design to make specialized models for agricultural spraying and dusting. In 1947, the helicopters received the first U.S. government certificate ever issued to a dedicated agricultural aircraft. At about the same time, Hiller, another helicopter company, promoted the use of its new helicopters for "air farming" at agricultural trade shows.[1]

Helicopters cannot fly as fast as airplanes or carry as heavy a load, but they can work in smaller spaces and apply chemicals more precisely. Their rotors make a swirling downwash that coats the undersides of leaves as well as the tops.

Helicopters were also useful to prevent frost and moisture damage to fruit crops. The rotor downwash could blow away cold, frost-forming air close to the ground. It could also help dry out rain-soaked fruit to prevent spoilage.[2]

Whether they fly airplanes or helicopters, agricultural pilots today continue to help farmers produce the food we eat. Although fewer ag pilots are flying, they are doing more and shouldering bigger responsibilities than ever.

"The people who are doing it are no longer daredevil, fly-by-night, hotshot pilots," says Robert McCurdy, who began flying ag planes more than thirty years ago. "These guys are flying anywhere from half-million- to million-dollar airplanes. These guys are intelligent, they're educated. . . . We're a whole lot more professional than we were in the past."[3]

And they continue to fly for the joy of working with the earth and flying close to it. Joe Vick continues the ag flying business his father started in the late 1940s. He also farms about three hundred acres of his own near Columbus, Ohio. "I've enjoyed it," he says. "I really feel fortunate that I've been able to combine the two things I'm most interested in, my flying and the agriculture."[4]

Chapter Notes

Chapter 1. A Flash of Wings

1. Author interview with Robert McCurdy, April 18, 2000.

2. Southern Plains Agricultural Research Center, U.S. Department of Agriculture, "Aerial Application Technology for Crop Protection," n.d., <http://scrl.usda.gov/scrl/apmru/aerial/intro.htm> (June 22, 2000).

3. Author interview with Lynn Carlson, May 5, 2000.

4. Southern Plains Agricultural Research Center.

5. General Aviation Manufacturers Association, *1999 Databook* (Washington, D.C.: General Aviation Manufacturers Association, 2000), p. 10.

6. Carlson.

7. Southern Plains Agricultural Research Center.

8. David Pimentel, "Is Silent Spring Behind Us?" *Silent Spring Revisited* (Washington, D.C.: American Chemical Society, 1987), p. 175.

9. Rachel Carson, *Silent Spring* (New York: Houghton Mifflin, 1962), p. 156.

10. Letter from Ivan W. Kirk, July 18, 2000.

11. Carlson.

Chapter 2. The Crop Dusters

1. Mabry I. Anderson, *Low & Slow: An Insider's History of Agricultural Aviation* (Clarksdale, Miss.: Low & Slow Publishing, 1986), pp. 5–7.

バ

2. Roger E. Bilstein, *Flight in America: From the Wrights to the Astronauts* (Baltimore: Johns Hopkins University Press, 1984), p. 66; National Agricultural Aviation Museum, brochure (Jackson, Miss.: National Agricultural Aviation Museum, undated).

3. Boeing Co., "Stearman Kaydet Trainer," *A Brief History,* © 2000, <http://www.boeing.com/companyoffices/history/boeing/kaydet.html> (July 3, 2000).

4. Federal Aviation Administration, *Pilot's Handbook of Aeronautical Knowledge* (Washington, D.C.: U.S. Government Printing Office, 1997), pp. 2:6, 2:7.

5. William K. Kershner, *The Student Pilot's Flight Manual* (Ames, Iowa: Iowa State University Press, 1979), pp. 3–4.

6. Ibid., p. 109.

7. William Schweizer, *The Ageless Ag-Cat* (Bluffton, S.C.: Rivilo Books, 1995), pp. 3–5.

8. Jim Avis and Martin Bowman, *Stearman: A Pictorial History* (Osceola, Wis.: Motorbooks, 1997), p. 88.

9. National Agricultural Aviation Museum.

10. Author interview with Robert McCurdy, April 18, 2000.

11. Red Baron Pizza, *Red Baron Pizza: The Official Website of the Sky,* "Not Your 'Plane' Old Aircraft," n.d., <http://www.redbaron.com/planes.htm> (July 8, 2000).

12. Gunston, Bill, *World War II United States Aircraft* (London: Leisure Books Ltd., 1985), p. 16.

Chapter 3. Designed for the Job

1. Author interview with Robert McCurdy, April 18, 2000.

2. Author interview with Joe Vick, May 19, 2000.

3. McCurdy.

4. Vick.

Chapter 4. The Modern Ag Plane

1. Author interview with Luther Gibbs, Sr., May 6, 2000.

2. Author interview with Luther Gibbs, Jr., July 11, 2000.

3. Donald S. Lopez, *Aviation: A Smithsonian Guide* (New York: Macmillan, 1995), p. 244.

4. William Schweizer, *The Ageless Ag-Cat* (Bluffton, S.C.: Rivilo Books, 1995), p. 96.

5. Author interview with Robert McCurdy, April 18, 2000.

6. Ibid.

7. Kristin Snow, answers to author's questions via e-mail, June 30, 2000.

8. Air Tractor Inc. sales literature.

Chapter 5. Helicopters

1. Jay P. Spencer, *Whirlybirds: A History of the U.S. Helicopter Pioneers* (Washington, D.C.: University of Washington Press, 1998), pp. 218, 318.

2. Ibid., p. 429.

3. Author interview with Robert McCurdy, April 18, 2000.

4. Author interview with Joe Vick, May 19, 2000.

Glossary

Ag-Cat—A biplane designed by Grumman for agricultural aviation.

agriculture—The production of crops and livestock.

Air Tractor—A family of agricultural airplanes, and the name of the company that manufactures them.

biplane—An airplane with two sets of wings.

crop duster—An old-fashioned term for an agricultural pilot.

dust—In crop dusting, an agricultural chemical in a dry, powdered form.

GPS—Global Positioning System. A network of U.S. satellites that transmits radio signals for navigation.

hangar—A building made for storing aircraft.

hopper—A container with an opening usually at the bottom from which the contents can be emptied at a specific rate.

lift—The force that lifts an aircraft into the air.

radial engine—An engine with cylinders arranged in a circular pattern around a central crankshaft.

stall—The loss of a wing's lifting ability.

Stearman—A biplane built by the thousands during World War II to train military pilots and later used for crop dusting and other purposes.

turboprop engine—An engine that uses exhaust gases to spin a turbine that turns a propeller.

Further Reading

Avis, Jim, and Martin Bowman. *Stearman: A Pictorial History*. Osceola, Wis.: Motorbooks, 1997.

Ayres, Carter M. *Pilots and Aviation*. Minneapolis: Lerner, 1990.

Bilstein, Roger E. *Flight in America: From the Wrights to the Astronauts*. Baltimore: Johns Hopkins University Press, 1984.

Lopez, Donald S. *Aviation: A Smithsonian Guide*. New York: Macmillan, 1995.

Mackie, Dan. *Flight*. Burlington, Ontario: Hayes Publications, 1986.

Spencer, Jay P. *Whirlybirds: A History of the U.S. Helicopter Pioneers*. Washington, DC: University of Washington Press, 1998.

Yount, Lisa. *Women Aviators*. New York: Facts on File, 1995.

Internet Addresses

Air Tractor, Inc. n.d. <http://www.airtractor.com>.

Lavender, Graham. *AgAir Update*. April 11, 2001. <http://www.agairupdate.com>.

Welcome to National Agricultural Aviation Association. © 2000. <http://www.agaviation.org>.

Index

A
Ag-Cat, 22–28, 37
agricultural aviation, 6, 9, 11, 12, 22, 35
Air Tractor
    AT-400, 33–35
    AT-802A, 37, 39
    AT-802F, 37, 39
Automatic Flagman, 25

B
Bell Helicopter, 41
Boeing Company, 15

C
Carlson, Lynn, 8–9, 11
Carson, Rachel, 10
crop dusters, 12–13, 16, 19–20
Curtiss JN-6H Jenny, 13

D
Darmoy, Etienne, 13–14
Delta Aero Dusters, 15
Delta Air Lines, 15
dry chemicals, 12, 13, 16

F
flaggers, 25

G
general aviation, 9
Gibbs, Luther, Jr., 29–30, 32–35
Gibbs, Luther, Sr., 29–30, 32–33
Global Positioning System (GPS), 26
Grumman Aircraft Corporation, 22–23, 28

H
helicopters, 6, 9, 40–41
Hiller, 41
hopper, 13, 15, 16, 24, 25, 28, 30, 32, 33–34, 35, 37, 39
Huff-Daland Aero Corporation, 15

J
jet engine, 34–35

K
Kirk, Ivan W., 11

L
lift, 17, 19, 25, 40

M
Macready, John, 13–14
McCook Field, 13
McCurdy, Robert, 7, 20, 22, 27, 35, 37, 42

N
National Agricultural Aviation Association, 8–9
National Agricultural Aviation Museum, 19

P
peregrine falcon, 10
piston engine, 15, 34–35

R
radial engine, 15, 19, 27, 37
Red Baron Pizza Squadron, 20

S
Snow, Kristin, 37
spray boom, 16
stall, 17, 19, 28, 39
Stearman, 15–17, 19–20, 21, 22, 23

T
turboprop engine, 34–35, 37

U
U.S. Department of Agriculture, 11, 12–13, 14

V
Vick, Joe, 24–25, 26, 42

W
wildfires, 37
World War I, 13
World War II, 9, 15, 40